Wild Flowers of Mountain and Moorland
by Roger Phillips

assisted by Martyn Rix
and Jacqui Hurst

Elm Tree Books London

G000245781

INTRODUCTION

We have aimed to photograph and describe 120 of the most conspicuous plants found growing on mountain and moorland in the British Isles and northern Europe.

How to use this book ˋ

The flowers are arranged roughly in order of flowering, from spring to autumn. One photograph shows the most important part of the plant, laid out so that the details can be seen easily and clearly. The other shows the same plant (or a related or similar one) growing, and gives some idea of its habitat, height, bushiness and stiffness. Where two species are shown, the differences between them are mentioned in the text.

What and where is mountain and moorland?

Moorland forms in those parts of the British Isles with very sandy soils, or which have hard, lime-free rock such as granite or sandstone near the surface. The acid soils which form in these areas have characteristic wild flowers. Because these soils are very bad for agriculture, they have remained uncultivated and usually not even enclosed, so they are now popular as holiday areas for walkers and lovers of open spaces. The New Forest, Dartmoor, Exmoor and Bodmin Moor, North Wales, the Lake District, and most of the mountains of Scotland and Ireland are examples of areas where much of the land is covered by heathland or moorland. On drier soils, heathers (page 124–132) and bracken (page 154) are the dominant plants; on wetter soils, Moor Grass (page 72) and Sphagnum Moss (page 152) are dominant.

Heather and Lady's Mantle in Scotland

In other areas, on limestone with heavy rainfall, on clay soils or in shallow lakes, small bogs may form, and acid soil may develop. Extensive areas of raised bog have been formed in central Ireland, although the underlying rock is mainly limestone. These bogs are exploited for peat by Bord na Mona, the peat board for turf fuel, which is made into brickettes, and for garden peat. This so-called moss peat is composed of the dead remains of Sphagnum Moss, Cotton Grass and heather. Sedge peat, which comes mostly from Somerset, is blacker and less spongy, and is composed mainly of the remains of hedges and rushes.

Other major areas of acid soils are found in Sussex, Surrey and Hampshire from Tunbridge Wells to Aldershot, around Bournemouth, and on Purbeck; on the coasts of Devon and Cornwall especially on the Lizard peninsula, on the Breckland in Suffolk, and parts of the Pennines. On the Continent, most of Scandinavia has acid soils, and areas of heathland are found in eastern Holland and north Germany in the Black Forest, in Brittany, in Les Landes near Bordeaux, and in north-western Spain and Portugal.

The photographs
The studio photographs were taken on a Bronica 120 format with a 75 mm lens. Scale: ○ is 1 cm. The field photographs were taken on a Nikon FM camera with a 50 mm lens, occasionally with close-up attachments. The film was Kodak Ektachrome 64 ASA in both cases, but when used outdoors it was pushed one stop in development.

Glossary

calyx	outer, usually green, parts of flower
cleistogamous	specialised, usually very small flowers which set seed without opening
corolla	inner, usually coloured, parts of flower
glume	one of the chaff-like bracts which form the calyx in the inflorescence of grasses and sedge
oblanceolate	a rounded spear-shape
pappus	the downy appendage on certain fruits or 'seeds'
peduncle	the primary stalk of an inflorescence
scabrid	rough-surfaced
stamen	the fertilising organ of the plant, consisting of the anther and filament
staminode	the stamen without its anther
style	the section of the female parts which connect the ovary with the stigma
stolon	underground shoot producing new plant

Creeping Willow photographed May 18

Creeping Willow

Salix repens (Willow family) is a small shrub, distributed all over the British Isles, being commonest in Scotland; it is also found throughout Europe, and across Asia.

Subspecies *repens* and *argentea* can be told apart by the leaves which in *repens* are silky on the underside only, while in *argentea* they are silky on both sides, and by the catkins which are larger in *argentea*. They have creeping stems, varying in height from 30–150 cm, bearing catkins in April to May. *Repens* is found on damp heaths, while *argentea* colonises dune-slacks and occasionally rocky heaths in northern Scotland.

Other common willows include the **Eared Sallow**, *Salix aurita*, a shrub 1–2 metres high which is particularly common on the acid and boggy soils of Scotland and the west coast of Ireland; it is also found in southern Europe.

The Grey or Common Sallow, *Salix cinerea*, is very common in Britain and northern Europe and is found as a shrub or tree up to 10 metres high.

Creeping Willow (top left), Eared Willow (top right), Sallow (bottom)

Marsh Pennywort photographed May 20

Marsh Valerian

Valeriana dioica (Valerian family) is a low-growing perennial 15–30 cm
high which grows in marshy meadows, bogs and fens. It is scattered
throughout England and Wales and is also found in Scandinavia and
northern Europe as far east as central Russia. The male and female flowers
are borne on different plants, the male being twice the diameter of the
female, and appear in May and June.

Marsh Pennywort, *Hydrocotyle vulgaris*, also likes damp areas, being
found in marshes (sometimes actually floating in water), bogs, fens and
dune slacks; it is most common where the soil is slightly peaty. Large
numbers of conspicuous, round leaves arise from creeping stems, while
the very small and rather insignificant flowers, which are borne from June
to August, are hidden beneath them. Marsh Pennywort is quite common
throughout the British Isles and is also found in Europe as far east as the
Caspian Sea; it is also found in Algeria and Morocco.

6

Marsh Valerian photographed May 2

Bitter Vetch photographed May 14

Bitter Vetch

Lathyrus montanus (Pea family) is a perennial vetch, with creeping and tuberous rhizomes and flowering stems up to 40 cm high, with red flowers, fading to purple, from April to July. It has no tendrils. It is usually found on rough grassy slopes, on hillsides among heather and in open woods. It is found throughout the British Isles but is commonest in the Weald, the west and the north, and rare or absent in much of East Anglia. In Europe it is found everywhere except for the extreme south-east.

Vicia orobus, also called Bitter Vetch, is a much rarer plant, found quite frequently in rocky places and woods in Wales, but very rarely elsewhere from Devon and Gloucestershire to the Lake District, southern Scotland and up the west coast as far north as Sutherland; it is very rare in Ireland.

It differs from *Lathyrus montanus* in having white, purple-tinged flowers in racemes of 6–20, and 6–15 pairs of leaflets. It is confined to western Europe from Norway to Portugal, and in the Jura.

8

Bitter Vetch

Heath Milkwort photographed near Pitlochry

Heath Milkwort

Polygala serpyllifolia (Milkwort family) is a creeping perennial, very similar to the Common Milkwort, *Polygala vulgaris*, from which it can be distinguished by being usually smaller, with opposite, not alternate lower leaves, and by its habitat of lime-free heaths, moors and mountain-sides.

It is a variable plant, capable of producing its tiny flowers from May to August in many colours (notably pink and white) in addition to the usual blue. It is widely distributed throughout the British Isles, being commonest in Scotland and on the west coast, and scarcer in parts of East Anglia and the Midlands. In Europe it is found from south-west Norway and the Pyrenees as far east as Czechoslovakia. The name milkwort refers to the milky juice found in the roots; at one time the plant was supposed to increase the milk yield from cows, but this has never been proved.

Heath Milkwort photographed May 9

Broom photographed in Brittany

Broom

Cytisus (Sarothamnus) scoparius (Pea family) is an erect shrub which grows up to 2 metres high, and is a familiar sight on heaths and hillsides. It prefers dry, sandy soil, strongly disliking chalk, and is widely distributed throughout the British Isles, with the exception of Shetland and Orkney. It is also found in Europe from Spain (including Madeira and Tenerife), north to Scandinavia and east as far as Poland and Hungary.

In earlier times the green twigs of broom were used for sweeping, thus giving rise to the household 'broom'. Broom tops were used as a diuretic, and broom buds (borne from March to June) are edible, being used in salads, pickled, or when open, to make a curious flower wine. If intending to eat broom buds be sure to distinguish between our native shrub and *Spartium junceum*, a similar species, which has become naturalised in southern England, as the latter is poisonous. *Spartium* has larger, paler flowers and round, smooth twigs; it normally flowers later than *Cytisus*, from June to August.

12

Broom photographed May 18

Pale Butterwort photographed May 16

Pale Butterwort

The butterworts are a family of small, insectivorous perennials, with sticky glandular leaves which were formerly used to curdle milk, hence the common name. *Pinguicula lusitanica*, the Pale Butterwort, occurs in south-west England, the west coasts of Ireland and Scotland, and western France, Spain, Portugal and Morocco. From this distribution it can be seen that *Pinguicula* prefers damp areas and indeed it is found on wet, acid heaths and moorland. The delicate, pale mauve flowers, borne from June to October, are self-pollinated. *P. lusitanica* grows to only about 10 cm tall, whereas *P. vulgaris*, **Common Butterwort**, is larger, reaching about 15 cm; it also flowers earlier, from May to July and is pollinated by small bees. It is found throughout Britain, being rare in the south, but common in Scotland, Wales and north-west Ireland, where it grows on bogs and peaty heaths and among wet rocks. It is also found in western Europe, northern Asia, North America and north Morocco.

14

Common Butterwort photographed June 3

Heath Dog-violet photographed April 2

Heath Dog-Violet

Viola canina (Violet family) is a low-growing perennial, up to 30 cm, found on heathland often in company with *V. riviniana* (Common Dog-Violet see page 18), from which it differs in having bluer flowers and fleshier narrower, less-toothed leaves.

There are several different forms of *V. canina* itself, all of which flower from April to June, and two named subspecies, *canina* and *montana*. The first of these has deep or bright blue flowers and is found on dunes, heath and dry grassland as well as fens, and is often very variable. It is scattered throughout the British Isles and is found in Europe from Scandinavia to central Spain, Portugal and east to northern Italy; it is also known in north-west Asia, Greenland and occasionally central Asia.

Pale Heath Violet, *V. lactea*, differs from both these subspecies in having pale greyish-violet flowers. It grows on acid heaths in western Europe from Ireland south to Portugal.

16

Heath Dog-violet

Common Dog-violet photographed April 20

Common Dog-Violet

Viola riviniana (Violet family) is a common perennial, growing up to about 20 cm, which is found on grass heaths, chalk downs, old pastures, mountain-sides, hedges and deciduous woodland. It is widely distributed throughout the British Isles, and is also found in all parts of Europe with the exception of the south-west. It will grow on all types of soil but dislikes extremely wet conditions; there are two subspecies, *riviniana*, which is found in the more sheltered places, and *minor*, which colonises the more exposed areas. Both produce flowers on side shoots arising from a central, non-flowering rosette, from April to June, and occasionally again in autumn.

All violets also produce, after the normal open flowers, a crop of cleistogamous flowers, which never open but still produce seed. As a result, many (usually sterile) hybrids are produced between the different violets, *V. riviniana* crossing freely with both *canina* and *lactea*.

Common Dog-violet

Bog Violet photographed June 6

Bog or Marsh Violet

Viola palustris (Violet family) is a small perennial with a creeping underground stem from which the shiny, heart-shaped leaves and pale (occasionally white) flowers are thrown up. As the common name implies, *V. palustris* inhabits acid bogs and marshy places in woods, often being associated with Sphagnum Moss. The open flowers appear from April to July, and these are pollinated by small bees; a later crop of cleistogamous flowers (see previous page) is also produced.

V. palustris is common in the northern and western (and therefore wetter) areas of the British Isles, and is also found throughout most of Europe although it is much less common in the south and east. There are two subspecies, *palustris*, which is the commoner of the two, and *juressi*, which is scattered throughout the British Isles, Ireland, and western Europe. *Juressi* generally grows alongside ssp. *palustris* and is connected with it by a number of intermediate forms.

Bog Violet

Water Avens photographed in Scotland June 12

Marsh Cinquefoil

Potentilla palustris (Rose family) sometimes called *Comarum palustre*, is a creeping perennial which forms large patches in very wet bogs or in swamps on the edges of ponds and lakes, flowering from May to July. The stems reach 45 cm; the leaves are strikingly bluish-green with 5 or 7 leaflets; the petals are small and deep purple. Marsh Cinquefoil is found throughout the British Isles but is now rare in parts of south and central England, much of its former habitat having been drained. It is found as far south as Bulgaria and all round the northern hemisphere.

Water Avens, *Geum rivale* (Rose family), is similar in general appearance but grows mainly by rivers or streams, or on damp roadsides or meadows. From May to September it has nodding flowers (with orange-brown petals) on stems up to 60 cm high which are visited especially by bumble bees. Water Avens is found throughout the British Isles but is commonest in the north, and throughout Europe except for the far south. It is also found in Siberia and in North America.

Marsh Cinquefoil photographed in Finland July 3

Lesser Spearwort photographed June 9

Lesser Spearwort

Ranunculus flammula (Buttercup family) is a perennial which is very commonly found in wet areas throughout the British Isles; it inhabits bogs, the edges of streams and ponds, marshes, fens and wet woodlands. The flowers are borne from May to September and are pollinated by small flies and bees. A subspecies *minimus*, which often forms dense mats, is found in exposed areas by the sea in northern Scotland, the Outer Hebrides, Orkney and Shetland. Another subspecies, *scotica*, inhabits the shores of lakes in Argyll and the Inner Hebrides; it has also been recorded in County Mayo. *R. flammula* itself is found also in southern Europe, temperate parts of Asia and the Azores.

Similar to ssp. *minimus* is *R. reptans*, which is an even smaller and more delicate creeping plant of arctic lake shores in northern and central Europe.

Lesser Spearwort

Heath Bedstraw photographed June 18

Heath Bedstraw

Galium saxatile (Madder family) is a small creeping perennial with stems up to 20 cm long, which grows everywhere on dry, acid soil, often creeping through the fine grasses on the edges of patches of bracken. It flowers from June to August. The leaves on the flowering shoots are usually rather rounded or oblanceolate and by this it is distinguished from the rarer but similar *G. pumilum* and *G. sterneri*, both usually found on chalk or limestone, which have linear-lanceolate leaves. Heath Bedstraw is found throughout the British Isles and in Europe from Norway south to Spain and Portugal and eastwards to north-west Russia, and across the Atlantic in Newfoundland.

Lady's Bedstraw, *G. verum*, is also sometimes found on slightly acid soils. It is easily recognised by its yellow flowers and narrow leaves.

G. mollugo is similar in general appearance to *G. saxatile* but is much larger with stems usually more than 30 cm long. It grows in rough grass and hedges.

26

Lady's Bedstraw (left) Heath Bedstraw (right)

Sheep's Bit Scabious photographed in Cornwall June 25

Sheep's Bit Scabious

Jasione montana (Campanula family) is a small biennial or annual up to 50 cm tall, with a rosette of basal leaves and one or more stems topped by a fluffy head of about 50 small, pale blue flowers. It is found throughout the British Isles, but is much commoner in the south and west, and is almost absent from northern and eastern Scotland.

Its usual habitat is on sandy soils inland, or on rocky cliffs along the coast, but it is also common on stable sand dunes or coastal shingle; it flowers from May to August.

Sheep's Bit is found throughout Europe and in Morocco. Three varieties are recognised in Britain; var. *montana* with few, usually two flowering stems, and lanceolate leaves, is found in most habitats; var. *litoralis* with many stems and very narrow linear leaves grows on sand dunes and sandy places inland; and var. *latifolia* with few stems, broader lanceolate-spathulate leaves, and large flower heads with broad bracts, grows on cliff tops and rocky places near the sea.

Sheep's Bit Scabious

Trailing Tormentil

Common Tormentil

Potentilla erecta (Rose family) is very common on all acid soils throughout Britain and Europe, with the exception of the Mediterranean region where it is scarce. The rosette of leaves often withers and dies before flowering time. Several flower stems, from 10–30 cm tall, appear, bearing flowers from June to September.

P anglica, **Trailing Tormentil**, is similar to *P. erecta* but differs in that the rosette of leaves does not die off. The flowering stems are longer and creep along the ground, rooting at the nodes during late summer to produce new plants, rather in the same way that a strawberry does; the usually 4-petalled flowers are produced from June to September. *P. anglica* inhabits heaths, hedgerows and the edges of woods and is common throughout Ireland, Wales and parts of southern England.

P. reptans is also creeping, but differs in having always 5-petalled flowers and nearly always 5-lobed leaves.

Common Tormentil photographed May 26

Globe Flower photographed in Aberdeenshire August 6

Globe Flower

Trollius europaeus (Buttercup family) is a perennial which is common in Scotland (especially in the western Highlands) and fairly widely distributed throughout Wales and northern England, including the Lake District; it is occasionally seen in north-west Ireland. It tolerates both acid soils and limestone and is essentially a denizen of mountainous districts, being found in alpine pastures, by streams and in other damp, boggy places. The round flowers, appearing from June to August, are borne on a flower stem up to 60 cm high; tiny flies visit the flowers, acting both as pollinators and as aids to self-fertilisation. The Globe Flower is found throughout Europe, as far east as the Caucasus, and also in arctic America.

Globe Flower

Lesser Thyme-leaved Sandwort photographed June 12

Bog Stitchwort
Stellaria alsine (Carnation family) is a dwarf creeping perennial with shoots up to 40 cm long. The minute starry flowers about 6 mm across with 5 deeply-divided petals appear in May and June. Bog Stitchwort is common in wet bogs, often in trickling water or on bare mud throughout the British Isles; it is also found all round the northern hemisphere.

Lesser Thyme-leaved Sandwort, *Arenaria leptoclados* (Carnation family), is similar in scale, but grows in dry, sandy places where it can form large mats or a tiny plant depending on the season, as it is an annual. The flowers are 3–5 mm in diameter, with rounded petals. The closely-related *A. serpyllifolia* is commoner but occurs on all types of soil in open ground. It has large flowers 5–8 mm across, a larger, harder capsule and ovate not lanceolate sepals. Both flower from June to August. They are widely distributed on the Continent and in Asia.

Bog Stitchwort June 17

Petty Whin photographed in the Ardèche May 10

Petty Whin or Needle Furze

Genista anglica (Pea family) is a delicate gorse-like shrub up to 50 cm, with slender rather feeble prickles and small flat leaves, 2–8 mm long. It is found throughout England and Scotland but is completely absent from Ireland. On the Continent it is confined to western Europe, from northern Germany and Sweden to south-west Italy, Spain and Portugal. Petty Whin is found in wet or peaty heathland and on heather moors, often the first shrub to flower in May and June.

A second species of *Genista*, Dyer's Greenweed, *G. tinctoria*, is found in England, and as far north as southern Scotland, and is also absent from Ireland. It is commonest in rough grassland and on roadsides, often on clay soils, both acid and alkaline. It is easily distinguished by its leafy stems, the complete absence of spines, and by its late-flowering, from July to September.

Petty Whin

Hairy Greenweed photographed June 4

Hairy Greenweed

Genista pilosa (Pea family) is a prostrate shrub, without spines, up to 150 cm across. Its leaves are dark green, rounded and glabrous above, silky-hairy beneath. The flowers which appear in May and June are also silky. It grows on dry, acid rocks, on sea cliffs or acid sandy heathland. Hairy Greenweed is very rare in the British Isles. It is now found only on Ashdown Forest in Sussex, in Cornwall, especially on the Lizard peninsula and in Wales, in Pembrokeshire and Merioneth. Formerly it grew on the Breckland in East Anglia. On the Continent, however, it is widespread, from Denmark eastwards to Poland, and from central Spain to Bulgaria and Romania.

Hairy Greenweed

Ragged Robin photographed June (

Ragged Robin

Lychnis flos-cuculi (Carnation family) is a common plant of wet places, mainly on acid soils, but also in fens, by lakes and in damp meadows throughout the British Isles. It is a perennial forming a small tuft of narrow leaves from which the flowering stems, up to 75 cm tall, appear in May and June.

The flowers, which give the plant its name, are very distinct, each of the five petals being deeply cut into four narrow segments.

Ragged Robin is found throughout Europe, but is rare in the Mediterranean area. A second subspecies, ssp. *subintegra*, is found in the Balkan peninsula; it usually has white flowers and petals with only two lobes.

Ragged Robin

Wild Strawberry photographed May 21

Wild Strawberry

Fragaria vesca (Rose family) is a well-known perennial, being common throughout the British Isles, with the exception of northern Scotland where it is scarce. Strawberries tolerate a wide variety of soils, being found on sunny banks on acid soil and in woods on chalky soils, as well as scrub and grassland. It flowers from April to July and is visited by various insects; the characteristic fruits, which are minute compared to cultivated strawberries, appear during summer and early autumn.

The Alpine Strawberry, still grown today for its fruits, is a form of this species, although the common cultivated type is a cross of a species from Chile with one from North America. *F. vesca* is sometimes confused with the barren strawberry, *Potentilla sterilis*, and apart from the obvious differences in fruit (*P. sterilis* producing only a small head of dry nutlets) the two can be told apart by their petals, which in *Potentilla* are separated by obvious gaps. It is found throughout Europe.

Wild Strawberry

Heath Spotted Orchid photographed on the Lizard, Cornwall

Heath Spotted Orchid

Dactylorhiza maculata ssp. *maculata* (Orchid family) is widely distributed throughout Britain, although it is commonest in the north-west. It can be differentiated from the rather similar, but larger, Common Spotted Orchid, *D. fuchsii*, by the leaves which in ssp. *maculata* have smaller, lighter-coloured, almost circular spots, compared with the elliptical ones of *D. fuchsii*; the two spotted orchids hybridise freely, being pollinated by the same flies. Ssp. *maculata* prefers acid conditions, growing in habitats as diverse as dry heaths and moorlands and damp, marshy areas, even colonising sphagnum moss provided the latter is not too waterlogged.

In Scotland it is found on heather moors, and it occurs in moorland, grassland, and occasionally damp woodland margins in north-west England, west Wales, Cornwall, Devon and the New Forest; in Surrey, Sussex and Kent it is found on dry heathland. The Heath Spotted Orchid grows up to 60 cm (occasionally 80 cm) tall. The flowers which appear from early June to August vary in colour from very light pink to lilac-rose.

Heath Spotted Orchid photographed June 4

Cat's-foot, female plant photographed June 2

Cat's-foot

Antennaria dioica (Daisy family) is a dwarf perennial which forms mats of leaves and produces short (up to 20 cm) flowering stems in June and July. Male and female flowers are on different plants; the female flower heads are larger with pink, papery bracts, the male smaller with white bracts.

Cat's-foot is found most commonly in Scotland, the Lake District and in central Ireland, but occurs in England as far south as East Anglia and Cornwall, and in scattered localities in Wales.

It grows in short grass in dryish meadows, usually where the surface soil is poor, and often on the gravels of old glacial moraines. It is found both on acid soil and on limestone, especially in Ireland. Var. *hyperborea*, with white leaves, woolly on both sides, is known in the Hebrides, and similar forms are found in the Alps and the Caucasus.

On the Continent Cat's-foot is found from Spain to Bulgaria in the mountains, and at lower altitudes in the north. It also grows across Siberia and in North America.

Cat's-foot, male plant

Sheep's Sorrel photographed in Snowdonia

Sorrel

Rumex acetosa (Polygonum family) is an upright perennial, very common in damp meadows and marshes and bogs throughout the British Isles. The upright stems can reach 1 metre high and the bright pink flowers appear in May and June. Male and female flowers are found on separate plants. The stalked leaves are rather fleshy in texture and taste slightly acid. They can be used in salads and sauces in the same way as cultivated sorrel, *R. rugosus*, a plant unknown in the wild state, with larger, thinner leaves.

Sheep's Sorrel, *R. acetosella*, is a smaller plant, with creeping underground rhizomes, common on acid, sandy soils. It is usually not more than 20 cm high, with the leaf lobes spreading or pointing forewards.

Both species are found throughout Europe; *R. acetosa* also occurs in Asia and North America; *R. acetosella* in the temperate parts of both hemispheres.

48

Sheep's Sorrel photographed June 18

Scottish Asphodel

Scottish Asphodel photographed June 8

Tofieldia pusilla (Lily family) is a small perennial rush-like plant up to
20 cm tall, found on mountains from Yorkshire and Durham northwards.
It is commonest in the central and western Highlands and is found as high
as 1000 metres, and usually above 200 metres, growing in stony flushes and
by streams. The small white flowers open from June to August and are
followed by equally inconspicuous rounded green capsules. Outside the
British Isles, Scottish Asphodel is found all round the Arctic and in the
mountains of Europe, the Alps and the Carpathians.

Viviparous Bistort, *Polygonum viviparum* (Polygonum family), is also
commonest in northern England and Scotland, though known also in
north Wales and scattered along the west coast of Ireland. It grows in
mountain flushes and in both damp and rather dry meadows. The stem
reaches 30 cm high; the small flowers are usually confined to the upper part
of the inflorescence, the lower part is taken up with small purplish bulbils
which become detached and form new plants.

Viviparous Bistort photographed in Finland June 22

Northern Marsh Orchid photographed in Wensleydale, Yorkshire

Northern Marsh Orchid or Dwarf Purple Orchid

Dactylorhiza majalis ssp. *purpurella* (Orchid family) is a fairly small plant, generally growing up to 20 cm high and occasionally up to 40 cm. It can be distinguished from the closely related *D. majalis* by having leaves which are either unspotted or with relatively few spots clustered near the tips, whereas *D. majalis* has heavily spotted leaves. The flowers, which can range in colour from rose-pink to magenta or brilliant red-purple, appear from the middle of June to the end of July, and are insect pollinated. It prefers neutral or slightly acid soils and is found growing in company with rushes, sedges and bog asphodel in fens, bogs, marshes and other wet places, often at quite high altitudes. Ssp. *purpurella* is quite widely distributed through northern England and Scotland, north and west Wales, and parts of north, north-west and south-east Ireland. Hybrids frequently occur between ssp. *purpurella* and other orchids, notably *Gymnadenia conopsea* (see page 54) and *Dactylorhiza maculata* ssp. *maculata* (see page 44).

Northern Marsh Orchid photographed June 18

Small White Orchid photographed in Perthshire June 26

Small White Orchid

Pseudorchis albida (Orchid family) is a small, rather inconspicuous plant which usually only reaches a height of about 15 cm although occasionally it may grow as tall as 30 cm. It is found on grassy heaths and heathery areas, meadows and pastures in hilly districts, and although rare in southern and central Britain, it is quite common in western Scotland, Wales and parts of Ireland. *P. albida* flowers from mid-June to mid-July, the scented flowers attracting many insects such as bees, butterflies and flies.

The **Fragrant Orchid**, *Gymnadenia conopsea*, as the name suggests, also has scented flowers which attract butterflies and night-flying moths. It is found throughout Britain and Europe in heathy places, on chalk downs and limestone pasture. The flowers (usually pink, but sometimes white or magenta) are borne on a stem up to 45 cm tall during June to July. A variety, *densiflora*, the Marsh Fragrant Orchid, is larger and is found on fens and in marshes. Very occasionally hybrids between *G. conopsea* and *P. albida* are seen.

54

Fragrant Orchid

Lesser Butterfly Orchid photographed June 24

Lesser Butterfly Orchid

Platanthera bifolia (Orchid family) makes a plant from 25–50 cm tall. It is found scattered throughout Britain but is commonest in northern areas, particularly the north and west coasts of Scotland. It also occurs in the Lake District, Devon, Cornwall and Kent and is found throughout Ireland. The creamy-white, strongly scented flowers, borne from June to July, are pollinated by night flying moths, which also pollinate the related, but larger, Greater Butterfly Orchid, *P. chlorantha*.

P. bifolia is found on many different types of soil and in various habitats; it is common on heaths and moorlands, amongst heaths and heathers, but is more rarely found also on chalky soil, including chalk downland; it also occurs occasionally in woodland (especially beechwood) clearings. It is able to tolerate both dry and damp soils, sometimes growing alongside the common Marsh Orchid, although it particularly likes grassy meadowland in hilly districts.

Lesser Butterfly Orchid

Rhododendron photographed June 6

Rhododendron

Rhododendron ponticum (Heather family) is a tall shrub up to 10 metres, though usually about 3 metres, and is common on acid soils throughout the British Isles from southern England to western Ireland. It is naturalised in both these areas, spreading by seed which is very light and can be blown by the wind.

It is now native of south-western Spain and central and southern Portugal as well as Bulgaria and northern Turkey and the Caucasus, with an outlying station in the Lebanon, and was introduced to gardens in England in about 1775. It was widely planted both as an evergreen and as a rootstock onto which more colourful hybrids were grafted: the hybrids often died leaving the stock to grow.

Although *Rhododendron ponticum* is not now native of the British Isles, it grew here before the last ice age, about 20,000 years ago. Remains of it have been found in peat deposits near Gont in Western Ireland.

Rhododendron

Pignut photographed June 19

Pignut or Earthnut

Conopodium majus is common on heathy grassland throughout the British Isles. The plants grow a few basal leaves and a single flowering stem from an edible underground tuber about 3 cm across. Pignut flowers in May and June, often forming large colonies of single plants, in contrast to the similar but densely tufted Spignel.

Spignel, Baldmoney or Mew, *Meum athamanticum*, is a perennial up to about 60 cm high which is found in rough grassland in mountainous districts, flowering in June and July. It is commonest in Scotland from the southern uplands north-east as far as Aberdeen, where it is found in fields at the edge of the Dee. *M. athamanticum* is found in the mountains of western and central Europe.

Spignel – the flowers are going over, June 29

Lousewort photographed 23 July

Lousewort

Pedicularis sylvatica (Figwort family) is a perennial or biennial with an upright central flowering stem up to 15 cm high, but usually around 10 cm, and creeping side branches. It flowers from April to July, and grows on heathland, moorland and in rough meadows throughout the British Isles, though least commonly in central and eastern England. In Ireland, Scotland and Norway a hairy form, ssp. *hibernica* is often common, especially in wet bogs. Subspecies *sylvatica* is found also in central and western Europe.

Red Rattle, *Pedicularis palustris* is a taller plant, usually annual, with a single flowering stem up to 60 cm but usually around 20 cm. It is similar to Lousewort but has darker purplish-pink flowers with 4 teeth on the upper hooded petal and a hairy calyx. It grows in marshes and wet places and is common in the west and north of the British Isles, rarer in south-east and central England; it is found throughout Europe, except in the south-east. Other species of *Pedicularis* are common in the Alps and Pyrenees.

62

Lousewort (top), Red Rattle (bottom)

Alpine Lady's Mantle photographed June 27

Lady's Mantle

Alchemilla vulgaris (Rose family) is a very variable species, rare in southern and eastern England, but common elsewhere. In the largest species the stems reach 65 cm high, producing masses of tiny 4-petalled flowers from June to September. About 12 microspecies are recognised in the British Isles, but about 300 from the whole of Europe, differing in hairiness, the lobing of the leaves and the shape of the teeth, as well as size and habitat.

Alpine Lady's Mantle, *Alchemilla alpina*, is distinct from *A. vulgaris* in its leaves with 5–7 separate, narrow leaflets, silky beneath. It is commonest in the mountains in northern Scotland, by streams and on rocks and in short turf from sea level in the far north, up to over 1200 metres. It is also found in the Lake District, the Wicklow mountains and in a few localities in County Kerry. It can make dense mats of leaves with flowering stems up to 20 cm high, produced from June to August. It is found in the Arctic, the Pyrenees and the Alps, and also Greenland.

Lady's Mantle photographed June 1

Bogbean photographed June 12

Bogbean or Buckbean

Menyanthies trifoliata (Bogbean family) is common in wet marshes and bogs and in the shallow water of canals and lakes throughout the British Isles and in most of Europe. It is also found across Siberia and in North America and Japan. The leaves are divided into 3 oblanceolate leaflets and are reminiscent of those of broad bean, hence the English names.

The plant is perennial with stems that creep along the surface of the ground or float on the water. The flowering stem is from 15–30 cm in height, appearing from April until July. The flowers with their characteristic hairy petals are of two kinds, one with stamens longer than the style, the other with a long style and short stamens hidden in the flower, and are pollinated by insects. The rounded capsules contain large orange-brown seeds.

Bogbean

Bog Pimpernel photographed June 2c

Bog Pimpernel

Anagallis tenella (Primrose family) is a dwarf, creeping perennial found on wet heaths and damp meadows, and on seeping, peaty banks especially near the west coast throughout the British Isles. It is commonest in the New Forest, on Dartmoor and Exmoor and in Cornwall, in North Wales, the Lake District, the western isles of Scotland and in the west of Ireland. The round leaves are about 5 cm across and the flowers up to 14 mm in diameter, pink with darker veins, appearing from June to August. The stems root at the nodes as the plant creeps. In Europe Bog Pimpernel is found mainly in the west, as well as in North Africa, with one or two isolated stations in Greece, Crete and Sardinia.

Anagallis minima, Chaffweed, grows in somewhat similar habitats, often in bare, wet, sandy soil. It is a very small, erect, annual, from 1–4 cm tall, with minute white or pink flowers. It is found throughout the British Isles, but is commonest in Kent and Sussex, Dorset and Hampshire and on the west coasts. It is widespread in Europe, absent only from the far north.

Bog Pimpernel

Ivy-leaved Bellflower photographed July 2[...]

Ivy-leaved Bellflower

Wahlenbergia hederacea (Campanula family) is a small (up to 30 cm[...]
creeping perennial which is found on damp, acid heathland, by strea[...]
sides and in woodland clearings; the delicate flowers appear during Jul[...]
and August. In Britain *Wahlenbergia* inhabits Wales, parts of souther[...]
Ireland and is scattered throughout Hampshire, Sussex and Kent. I[...]
Europe it is found from Denmark south to Spain and Portugal and i[...]
south-western Yugoslavia.

    Heath Lobelia, *Lobelia urens* (Lobelia family), is a very rare perenni[...]
which grows up to 60 cm, and is found on grassy heathland and open place[...]
in chestnut coppice along the south coast of England from Cornwall t[...]
Sussex. *L. urens* continues to flower rather late in the season, from July t[...]
October; it is related to Water Lobelia, which grows in acid lakes i[...]
Scotland, the Lake District and Ireland and like this plant prefers damp[...]
acid soils. In Europe it is found in France, Spain, Portugal, the Azores an[...]
Madeira.

Heath Lobelia

Blue Moor Grass

Heathland Grasses

Wavy Hairgrass, *Deschampsian flexuosa*, syn. *Aira flexursa*, is common in open woods, on heathland and moorland throughout the British Isles. It grows in small tufts, with hair-like leaves and open panicles of silvery spikelets.

Mat-grass, *Nordus stricta*, is common on moorland and found also on heathland in the south, especially where there is heavy grazing by sheep. It forms dense tufts of wiry leaves and has one-sided narrow panicles of spikelets.

Sheep's Fescue, *Festuca ovina*, is a small tufted grass with very narrow and short panicles of small spikelets. It is common on all dry, well-drained soils.

Blue Moor Grass, *Molinia caerulea*, is a large tufted grass with broad bluish green leaves, and wiry flowering stems in late summer. It grows in wet bogs and peaty hillsides, producing beautiful autumn colour on hills in the west of the British Isles.

Blue Moor Grass (left), Mat-grass (centre), Wavy Hairgrass (right)

Yellow Sedge photographed July 8

Heathland Sedges

Sedges may be recognised by their triangular stems, and flat often rough-edged leaves. Male and female flowers are distinct, and usually on separate spikes. Most species are found in wet places.

Yellow Sedge, *Carex demiosa*, is also yellowish green. The flowering stems are often flat on the ground. The female spikes are widely separated, with long leaf-like bracts.

Star Sedge, *Carex echinata*, is common in wet places forming small tufts. The whole plant is bright yellowish green; the female spikes, few-flowered, with nutlets arranged like a star, at the apex of the stem.

Common Sedge, *Carex nigra*, is common in wet places, usually on acid soils. The leaves are greyish-green; the glumes between the nutlets are blackish.

Pill-headed Sedge, *Carex pilulifera*, makes tufts on moorland and dry heathland. The female spikes are small; the nutlets minutely hairy.

74

(Left to right): Yellow Sedge, Star Sedge, Common Sedge, Pill-headed Sedge

Jointed Rush photographed July 6

Heathland Rushes

True rushes, *Juncus* species, have smooth, usually cylindrical stems and smooth leaves. Wood rushes, *Luzula* species, have flat, grass-like leaves with scattered hairs and cylindrical flowering stems.

Jointed Rush, *Juncus articulatus*, has leaves with tranverse divisions. It is very common in wet meadows and along streams in bogs.

Soft Rush, *Juncus effusus*, is the commonest large tufted rush with soft stems filled with white pith. It is found in wet places throughout the British Isles.

Many-headed Woodrush, *Luzula multiflora*, has the flowers clustered in a tight head at the top of the stem. It forms small tufts among heather.

Heath Rush, *Juncus squerrosus*, forms small dense tufts of wiry, tough leaves. It is commonest on moorland where grazing is heavy.

Soft Rush (left), Many-headed Woodrush (top), Heath Rush (bottom)

Bog Thistle

Bog Thistle photographed August 1

Cirsium dissectum (Daisy family) is found in wet meadows, bogs and marshes in the south and east of England, in south Wales and in Ireland, where it is commonest in the north and west. It is a perennial with long creeping underground stems and upright leaves about 20 cm tall. The flowering stems which are produced from June to August are about 50 cm high with a few small leaves above the middle. On the Continent Bog Thistle is confined to western Europe from Germany to Spain.

Melancholy Thistle, *Cirsium helenioides* (syn. *C. heterophyllum*), is a rather similar but larger plant, up to 100 cm, with a strangely complementary distribution. It is found only in the north and west of England, in North Wales and in Scotland with one locality in Ireland. Its large, drooping seed heads gave it its English name; the Latin name refers to the difference between the large, undivided basal leaves, 20–40 cm by 4–8 cm, and the well-developed, often pinnate stem leaves. It flowers in July and August and usually grows by streams in the hills, in open woods.

78

Melancholy Thistle photographed August 10

Marsh Willowherb photographed August

Marsh Willowherb

Epilobium palustre (Fuschia family) is a slender, elegant perennial up to 6
cm high, flowering in July and August. It is found throughout the Britis
Isles in marshes, bogs and all wet places on acid soil. In Europe it grow
everywhere except along the Mediterranean, and is found all round th
Arctic. It can be distinguished from other Willowherbs by its narrow
sessile stem-leaves, underground stolons and flowers in a nodding raceme

Often growing in similar places, especially in mountainous areas, is *E
nterterioides*, a native of New Zealand, with creeping, rooting stems wit
small rounded leaves and flower stems up to 7.5 cm.

Eyebright, *Euphrasia micrantha* (Figwort family), is one of the man
species found in the British Isles. It is rather tall and slender, branche
usually with purplish leaves and lilac or purple flowers. It grows alway
among heather (*Calluna*) and is found in the northern and western part o
the British Isles and in northern and central Europe, south to Spain.

Eyebright photographed July 29

Common Speedwell photographed June 2

Marsh Speedwell

Veronica scutellata (Figwort family) is a slender perennial up to 50 cm tall
which grows up through the grasses in marshes and by rivers and lakes,
flowering from June to August. It is found throughout the British Isles and
on the Continent in most of Europe and across Asia.

Common Speedwell, *Veronica officinalis*, is found in drier places, and is
a creeping perennial with oblong leaves 2–3 cm long, and dense upright
spikes of flowers. It grows on heaths, rough grassy banks, and in open
woods throughout the British Isles and in Europe, eastwards to Siberia.

Similar but smaller, is Thyme-leaved Speedwell, *Veronica serpyllifolia*.
Its leaves are hairless, pale green and only 1–2 cm long. The flowers are
fewer and paler, white with bluish lines in ssp. *serpyllifolia*, a lowland
plant, and larger and bluer in ssp. *humifusa* which is usually found in the
mountains of Wales, the Lake District, Scotland and continental Europe.

Marsh Speedwell photographed July 27

Cotton Grass or Hare's-tail, *E. vaginatum*, July 4

Cotton Grass or Bog-Cotton

The four *Eriophorum* species (Sedge family) in the British Isles are often a conspicuous sight on bogs or peaty mountains. The commonest is *E. angustifolium* which has several drooping spikelets at the top of a stalk up to 60 cm high. It has underground creeping stems and long narrow leaves. It grows in wet marshes as well as among heather, and bogs. *E. vaginatum* is almost as common but absent from much of south-east England. It forms stout tufts and has stems up to 50 cm high with a single, upright spikelet. It is very conspicuous in some parts of northern England and southern Scotland where it can be dominant on the moors. *E. scheuchzeri* from the Alps and Pyrenees has a single spikelet but creeping rhizomes.

The other two species are rarer; *E. latifolium* is similar to *E. angustifolium* but has broader, pale-green leaves, minutely scabrid peduncles and grows in tufts. It is commonest in flushes on mountains or in small bogs. *E. gracile* is a slender plant with creeping rhizomes, very narrow leaves and scabrid peduncles.

Common Cotton-grass, *E. angustifolium*, June 16

Slender St John's Wort

Slender St John's Wort

Hypericum pulchrum (St John's Wort family) is an erect perennial up to 60 cm high, but usually around 25 cm, distinguished by its stalkless, round leaves and red-tinged petals. It grows on heaths in rough meadows and on grassy banks on acid soils, throughout the British Isles but rarest in central England, flowering from June to August. In Europe it is found mainly in the north-west and down the Atlantic coast to Spain and Portugal.

Trailing St John's Wort, *Hypericum humifusum*, is a creeping perennial with a stem up to 20 cm long from a woody base. The leaves are elliptic or oblong and the flowers are small, around 10 mm in diameter, produced from June to September. It is found throughout the British Isles by woodland rides, on heaths and dry moors. In Europe it is found everywhere except in the far south and the Arctic. The similar but rarer *H. linarifolium*, with very narrow leaves, is found in dry, sunny places, in Devon, Wales, the Channel Islands and western Europe.

Trailing St John's Wort

Harebell or Scottish Bluebell photographed July 1?

Harebell (**Bluebell** in Scotland)

Campanula rotundifolia (Campanula family), one of the most delicate and beautiful of British wild flowers, is a perennial found throughout the British Isles, although it is rare in Devon, Cornwall, and south-east Ireland. The Harebell is remarkably adaptable to a variety of altitudes and soil conditions, being found from sea level to mountain tops, on short grass on both acid and limestone hills, heathland, rocks, dunes and lake shores. It often grows on poor, shallow soils, when it will reach a height of only 15 cm or so, but if growing in good soil in a sheltered position it can make a plant of up to 45 (or occasionally 60) cm. The flowers which appear from July to September are usually pale blue, but sometimes white forms are found, and in parts of Scotland the blue is more intense. The flower heads droop, thus protecting the pollen from being washed away by rain; pollination is carried out by large bees and butterflies. Harebells are well adapted to exposed conditions: the wiry stems are able to withstand strong winds, and the rootstock is fine enough to creep into rock fissures.

Harebell or Scottish Bluebell

Bog Asphodel photographed July 7

Bog Asphodel

Narthecium ossifragum (Lily family) is a perennial, up to 40 cm, which is common in the high rainfall areas of north and west Britain, especially in Scotland; it is also found in Ireland and on acid heaths in Dorset, the New Forest and the Weald of Kent and Sussex. Bog Asphodel, as the name implies, prefers wet conditions and often grows in bog-moss, on wet moorland and heathland, and in damp, acid places on mountains. The striking flowers appear from July to September and are pollinated by small moths and flies; the resulting fruits, long, orange-red capsules, make a colourful sight on the bogs in autumn. *N. ossifragum* is found throughout northern and western Europe as far south as Portugal, and east to Sweden.

Bog Asphodel

Grass of Parnassus photographed near Wast Water

Grass of Parnassus

Parnassia palustris (Grass of Parnassus family) is a beautiful perennial with flowering stems up to 30 cm high, produced from July to September. The radical leaves are heart-shaped, on upright stalks, and there is one stalkless leaf about half way up the stem.

The flowers are visited mainly by hover flies. There are five normal stamens, and five staminodes which end in a fan of glistening stalked glands. These attract the flies initially but they soon move to the nectar produced on the flat base of the staminodes, and come in contact with the stamens.

Grass of Parnassus grows in wet bogs, by streams and flushes in hilly areas and on cliffs, in damp grassy places and on the stony shores of lakes, on both acid and alkaline soils. It is rare in England and Wales, except in parts of East Anglia, Derbyshire and Anglesey, but common in Lancashire and the Lake District, western Scotland and central and western Ireland.

Grass of Parnassus photographed July 12

Marsh Thistle photographed July

Marsh Thistle

Cirsium palustre (Daisy family) is very common in wet meadows, marshes
grassy bogs and on hillsides throughout the British Isles. It often reaches
metres in height and flowers from June to September. It is a biennial
making a flat rosette of leaves in the first year, and flowering the second
The flower heads are 1–1.5 cm in diameter. In the lowlands the flowers ar
nearly always dark reddish-purple, but in the hills, especially in area
where fogs and low cloud are common, white-flowered forms becom
plentiful. An ingenious theory has been put forward to explain this: tha
pollinating bumble-bees see pale flowers more easily on dull days and s
they are more efficiently pollinated. Outside the British Isles, Mars
Thistle is common throughout Europe, except along the Mediterranean
and is found also in North Africa and western Asia.

Spear Thistle, *Cirsium vulgare*, is also common in hilly areas and i
grassy meadows. It is less tall, up to 150 cm, with longer spines, fewe
larger heads 2–4 cm in diameter, and unwinged stems.

Marsh Thistle

Lesser Skullcap photographed August 11

Yellow Bartsia

Parentucellia viscosa (Figwort family) syn. *Bartsia viscosa*, is a stickily hairy annual up to 50 cm high, which grows in grassy places, heaths and old dunes, flowering from June to October. It is rare in eastern England, being known only in a few places in Kent and Sussex and in Dorset, but common in Devon and Cornwall and on the coasts of Wales and Lancashire. In Ireland it is frequent in the south-west, and found also scattered in places along the west coast. In Scotland it is only known in Argyll.

Yellow Bartsia is common on the Continent, especially in the west, from France to Portugal, the Azores and around the Mediterranean.

The second species, *Parantucelia latifolia*, with much smaller reddish-purple flowers, is shorter but found in similar habitats, all round the Mediterranean, as far north as north-western France.

Lesser Skullcap, *Scutellaria minor*, is common in damp places and bogs in some parts of England and Wales especially in the New Forest and Dartmoor. It grows up to 15 cm high, and flowers from July to September.

96

Yellow Bartsia photographed near Cadiz

Field Gentian photographed August 25

Marsh Gentian

Gentiana pneumonanthe (Gentian family) is an extremely rare perennial which should not be picked. In Britain it is found only on wet heaths from Dorset to Sussex, in Anglesey, and parts of East Anglia and the Midlands. The flowers which are carried on stems of up to 40 cm tall, appear in August and September, and are pollinated by bumble-bees. *G. pneumonanthe* is also found scattered throughout much of Europe but is particularly rare in the south.

The Field Gentian, *Gentianella campestris*, is common in Scotland and on the north-west coast of Ireland, quite widespread in the Midlands, northern England and Wales, and rare in southern England. It is a biennial, and grows from 10–30 cm tall, on heaths and grassland (usually on acid or neutral soil), and dunes. The flowers are produced from July to October and are self-pollinated or fertilised by bumble-bees, moths or butterflies. *G. campestris* grows throughout northern and central Europe.

Marsh Gentian photographed August 12

Wild Chamomile photographed July 10

Wild Chamomile

Chamaemelum nobile (Daisy family) is found in dry grassland on acid soils, usually where grazing is quite heavy; it is common only in southern England, especially on Dartmoor, Exmoor, the New Forest and Cornwall and in west Cork and south Kerry. In Europe it is native only in the west southwards to Spain, Portugal and North Africa but was traditionally grown in herb gardens and as a scented lawn, so has become naturalised elsewhere. It is a perennial, with creeping and rooting non-flowering stems, and flowering stems about 15 cm long, usually little-branched, appearing from June to August.

Most other Chamomile and related genera are annuals, or much larger perennials with much broader flower stems, and larger flowers.

Wild Chamomile

Common Sundew

Sundew

The Sundews are insectivorous perennials, with sticky, glandular leaves and small white flowers which open only in hot sun; they are usually self-pollinated. The leaves digest small flies which are trapped on the sticky hairs. **Common Sundew**, *Drosera rotundifolia*, is the commonest of the three European species being found throughout Scotland, the north of England, Wales and western Ireland, and scattered throughout southern England. It makes a plant from 6–25 cm tall, flowering from June to August. It inhabits bogs and wet peaty places on moors and heathland, often growing in Sphagnum Moss throughout Europe, with the exception of the Mediterranean region, northern Asia and North America.

Great Sundew, *Drosera anglica*, grows from 10–30 cm tall, flowering in July and August and is usually found in the wetter parts of bogs.

The similar **Long-leaved Sundew**, *Drosera intermedia*, usually grows in bare, peaty places. It is shorter (5–10 cm tall) with the flowering stem arising from the side of the rosette of leaves.

Great Sundew

Top: Lesser Twayblade photographed in the Peak District

Lesser Twayblade

Listera cordata (Orchid family) is a small, inconspicuous orchid, growing up to 15–20 cm tall, and often hidden from view under clumps of heather or other vegetation. It is scattered throughout the northern part of Britain, being common in south-west Scotland, and is also found in northern Wales, Irish coastal areas and the north coast of Devon. It prefers rather acid soil, and is often found growing on clumps of damp moss under heather on moorland hillocks and ridges; it also inhabits clearings in pine and other upland woods, and the plants growing in this latter habitat are usually more vigorous with larger leaves than the moorland ones.

L. cordata is normally a plant of hilly districts, being found at altitudes up to 800 metres in Scotland and Ireland, although in western Ireland it is also found almost at sea level. The flowers, which appear from June to September are either pollinated by minute flies and wasps or self-fertilised. It is found in Europe from Iceland and Scandinavia to the Pyrenees.

Lesser Twayblade photographed July 6

Crowberry photographed in fruit July 30

Crowberry

Empetrum nigrum (Crowberry family) is restricted to the north and west of England, Wales, Scotland and Ireland, and is common on moorlands and mountains. It makes a small evergreen shrub, up to 45 cm, and generally grows on dry, acid, peaty soils in exposed places, although it is also found in coniferous forest clearings. The insignificant, pink-purple flowers appear in May and June and are thought to be wind-pollinated. Crowberry is a very variable plant, and two subspecies are recognised; ssp. *nigrum*, which has red stems when young and is generally found at lower altitudes, and ssp. *hermaphroditum*, which has green stems when young, and broader leaves, and is restricted to Arctic regions and the mountains of northern Europe. As the name suggests, ssp. *hermaphroditum* bears flowers of both sexes on the same plant, while in ssp. *nigrum* male and female flowers are borne on separate plants. *Nigrum* is found in northern Europe and mountains, south as far as the Pyrenees and central Italy.

Crowberry

Dwarf Cornel photographed July 15

Dwarf Cornel

Cornus suecica syn. *Chamaeperilymenum suecicum*, is a dwarf plant with underground stems creeping through the moss and short upright stems up to 8 cm high with pairs of leaves, usually terminating in a flower head. The individual flowers are minute, about 2 mm long, about 10–20 in a head, surrounded by 4 whitish bracts. When fertilised the flowers form red, fleshy fruits 5 mm across.

Dwarf Cornel is common only in the highlands of Scotland, growing with heather and bilberry on grouse moors, and flowering in June and July. It is known also from the North Yorkshire moors and in one place in the Lake District. In Europe it is found in Scandinavia, Holland and North Germany, but not in the Alps. It is also found in Arctic Asia and North America.

Dwarf Cornel

Cloudberry in fruit photographed August 15

Cloudberry

Rubus chamaemorus (Rose family) is a low-growing (up to 20 cm) perennial, with far-creeping underground stems, found on mountain moors and
bogs in Scotland, the north of England and the Midlands, and in one or
two places in north Wales. The male and female flowers are borne on
separate plants from June to August, and these are pollinated by small flies
and bumble-bees. The fruits, which are red when they first appear, turn
orange when ripe, and are edible, but rather insipid. They are never very
frequent in Scotland and are usually eaten by grouse or other birds before
they are really ripe, but in Scandinavia they are found in large numbers
and used for making jam and cloudberry liqueur. Cloudberry is found
throughout northern Europe, as far south as north-west Czechoslovakia.

Cloudberry in flower photographed June 14

Raspberry in fruit photographed August 23

Raspberry

Rubus idaeus (Rose family) is a common shrub found throughout the British Isles (although it is scarcer in south-west Ireland) and cultivated for its fruit. It grows on woods and heaths, especially in hilly districts, and is particularly well-adapted to the long daylight hours found in northern districts; it is notable that Scotland is one of the centres of commercial raspberry growing, for which some of the many selected cultivars of the wild raspberry are used. In the wild, the stems grow from 100–150 cm tall, and the flowers, which are borne from June to August, are usually self-fertilised although they are occasionally pollinated by insects, including bees. The delicious fruits, which are normally red, but occasionally yellow, are popular not only with humans but also with birds who help to spread their seeds. *R. idaeus* is found throughout most of Europe, but only on mountains in the south.

Raspberry in flower

Bearberry in flower photographed May 20

Bearberry
Arctostaphylos uva-ursi (Heather family) is a dwarf, evergreen shrub, with long rooting, trailing branches bearing thick, leathery leaves which often form dense mats. In Britain it is restricted almost entirely to Scotland, where it is common, especially in the Highlands but it is also found scattered in a very few places in northern England and north-west and western Ireland. It is usually found on rather dry scree slopes, and on stony, gravelly moorland but is occasionally also seen in open woodland. The flowers which appear from May to July are self-fertilised, or pollinated by bumble-bees, and the fruits which have rather dry flesh and so are not good to eat, are borne from July to September. *A. uva-ursi* is found throughout most of Europe, with the exception of the extreme south.

Bearberry in fruit (unripe) photographed July 18

Cowberry in fruit photographed August 23

Cowberry or Red Whortleberry

Vaccinium vitis-idaea (Heather family) is a low, evergreen shrub (up to 30 cm) which is commonly found in Scotland; it is also scattered throughout northern England, as far south as Yorkshire and Leicestershire, Wales, Northern Ireland and in one or two places in Southern Ireland. It is adapted to exposed, rather dry conditions and is found on moors and in woods on acid soils up to an altitude of about 1000 metres. It flowers from June to August and is often self-fertilised, although it is also pollinated by bees and butterflies. The bright red fruits, which are edible, but rather acid and tasteless, appear from August to October. Birds like the berries and the seeds are spread in their droppings.

V. vitis-idaea is found in northern and central Europe, as far south as the northern Appennines, Albania and Bulgaria.

Cowberry in flower photographed June 23

Bilberry in flower May 25

Bilberry, Whortleberry or Huckleberry
Vaccinium myrtillus (Heather family) is a low-growing (up to 45 cm) shrub, which is common throughout the British Isles, although scarce in parts of East Anglia and the Midlands. It grows on heaths and moorland, and in open woodland on acid soils, up to an altitude of about 1300 metres. The flowers, which are produced from April to June, according to latitude, are occasionally self-fertilised, but are pollinated chiefly by bees, and the delicious, juicy, purple-black fruits appear from July to September. When eaten raw, the berries are rather acid, but they are delicious when cooked and used to make tarts, cheesecakes or summer pudding. In autumn the leaves of *V. myrtillus* turn a brilliant orange-red colour. The bilberry is found throughout most of Europe, but only on mountains in the south.

Bilberry in fruit August 20

Dwarf Cranberry photographed May 28

Cranberry

Vaccinium oxycoccos (Heather family) is a very dwarf (up to 5 cm) evergreen shrub, with fine, wiry stems which creep over the surface of the ground, often forming a dense carpet. It is fairly common in northern and central England, Wales, and eastern Ireland, but is rare in northern Scotland and southern England. The cranberry likes to grow in very wet peat bogs, often in Sphagnum Moss, and is also found on wet heathland. The minute flowers, which appear from June to August, are pollinated by small bees and flies; the fruits, which are edible, are produced from August to October, and are beloved of grouse and blackcock. *V. oxycoccos* is known throughout northern and central Europe, south to central France, northern Italy and south-eastern Russia.

Dwarf Cranberry, *V. microcarpum*, is similar to the common Cranberry but is smaller with leaves 3–8 mm long, and a berry 5–8 mm across. It is found in rather drier places and is commoner in the Scottish highlands.

Dwarf Cranberry

Large Birdsfoot-trefoil photographed July 17

Large Birdsfoot-trefoil

Lotus uliginosus is common on wet heaths, marshes, damp meadows and roadsides in the British Isles, though it is rare in northern Scotland. In Europe it is frequent almost everywhere.

It is larger than Common Birdsfoot-trefoil, *L. corniculatus*, with stems up to 1 metre long from a spreading root system which produces numerous stolons. It is usually hairy, and the calyx teeth point outwards when the flower is in bud, giving a characteristic bristly appearance to the young heads; these often hold drops of dew or rain, as shown here. The flowers are produced from June to September.

Large Birdsfoot-trefoil

Bell Heather photographed in Cornwall June 25

Bell Heather

Erica cinerea (Heather family) makes a small shrub up to 75 cm high, but usually around 30 cm; it is one of the three common heathers, found throughout the British Isles where the soil is suitable and so absent from large areas of central England and parts of the central plain of Ireland. It requires very acid, but rather dry peaty soil, and favours sunny banks, moorland and well-drained rocky soils, and rock ledges. The bell-shaped flowers are bright reddish-purple and this colour distinguishes it from Cross-leaved Heath (page 126) which has pale pink flowers. It is also earlier flowering than the other common heather, opening in June and lasting until September. On the Continent Bell Heather is confined to western Europe from Norway south to Spain and Portugal and as far east as Germany and Italy.

Bell Heather

Cross-leaved Heath photographed July 20

Cross-leaved Heath

Erica tetralix (Heather family) makes a low shrub up to 70 cm, but usually about 25 cm; it is common in suitable soils throughout the British Isles requiring wet, acid peat, and is usually less plentiful than the other two species. The umbels of pale pink, bell-shaped flowers from 5–9 mm long, distinguish it from all other species except the very rare Mackay's Heath, (page 130), which can be distinguished by having its leaves more crowded and standing out from the stem, not pointing upwards, and by having sepals which are glabrous not woolly beneath. (Cross-leaved Heath flowers from July to September – somewhat earlier than Ling, but it has a longer flowering season). On the Continent it is known from northern Europe eastwards to Latrica and Finland and in western Europe south to Spain and Portugal.

Cross-leaved Heath

Dorset Heath photographed August 2

Dorset Heath

Erica ciliaris (Heather family) is a low shrub up to 80 cm high, but usually around 30 cm, found in wet bogs and heathland in Dorset, where it is found in the Purbeck area, Devon, Cornwall, and in one place in Connemara. From June to September it produces large, pink flowers 8–12 mm long, which are arranged in an elongated raceme, not an umbel as with the flowers of Bell Heather. On the Continent it is found only down the Atlantic coast from France, Spain and Portugal.

Cornish Heath, *Erica vagans*, is confined in Britain to Cornwall where it is common on heaths and cliff tops on the Lizard peninsula. It flowers in July and August, and has small bell-shaped flowers and exerted anthers 0.5–0.8 mm long. It is confined to western Europe from France to central Spain. The very similar *E. multiflora* from the northern and western Mediterranean region is taller, with larger flowers 4–5 mm long and longer anthers 1–5 mm long. It often grows on limestone.

Dorset Heath (top) and Cornish Heath photographed August 1

Irish Heath photographed March 30

St Dabeoc's Heath

Daboecia cantabrica (Heather family) is a straggling shrub up to 70 cm tall often growing up through other bushes. Its large purplish-pink bell-shaped flowers, 9–14 mm long are produced from July to September. It differs from tone heathers in having alternate, not whorled leaves and a corolla which falls as it fades and does not remain attached to the flower when dead and brown. It is found only in Connemara in Ireland, in western France, northern Spain and Portugal. St Dabeoc was a Celtic saint who worked in Ireland and founded a priory on an island in Loughdery in County Donegal in about 550.

Mackay's Heath, *Erica mackaiana*, is known only from bogs in Connemara, County Donegal and the province of Orviedo in north-western Spain.

Irish Heath, *Erica erigena*, is known only from bogs and stream-sides in Connemara, County Donegal, north-west Spain and Portugal. It flowers in March and April on an upright shrub of up to 120 cm.

Mackay's Heath (left), St Dabeoc's Heath (right)

Ling or Heather photographed August 4

Ling, Heath or Heather

Calluna vulgaris (Heather family) is the commonest of the heathers in the British Isles, found everywhere on dry, acid soil, even on the tops of downs and in peaty pockets on limestone. It is a low shrub up to 50 cm flowering from July to October. True heathers, *Erica* species, have tubular or bell-shaped flowers, with small green sepals, while *Calluna* has open flowers with five large purple petal-like sepals and a smaller lobed corolla. The flowers are much visited by bees and other insects for pollen and nectar but are also pollinated by wind.

Ling is found throughout the British Isles and is the dominant plant on large areas of moorland. Its young shoots are the staple food of the red grouse. Outside the British Isles it is much rarer and seldom found in such quantity, though known through most of Europe except for the south-east, in Morocco and the Azores.

Ling or Heather

Meadow-sweet photographed August 6

Meadow-sweet

Filipendula ulmaria (Rose family) is a perennial which grows from 50–200 cm tall. Numerous sweetly-scented flowers are produced from June to September, and these are self-pollinated, and also visited by numerous insects, including midges and craneflies. Meadow-sweet is common throughout the British Isles, with the exception of parts of northern Scotland where it is relatively rare, and is found in swamps, marshes, fens, damp woodland and meadows and wet rock ledges. In former times Meadow-sweet was valued for the pleasant scent of its foliage, and was used as a strewing herb; the flowers were also used to flavour mead, while the leaves were added to wines and preserves. Meadow-sweet is common throughout Europe, with the exception of the Mediterranean region.

Meadow-sweet

Bog Myrtle photographed July 26

Bog Myrtle or Sweet Gale

Myrica gale (Bog Myrtle family) is a deciduous shrub which grows from 60 to 250 cm tall, and spreads by means of suckers. It is common throughout western and central Scotland, western and central Ireland, the Lake District, north-west Wales, Cornwall and Dorset, and is scattered in a few other areas of the British Isles. Bog Myrtle grows, as the name suggests, in bogs, fens, lake shores and on wet heathland. The male and female catkin are somtimes borne on separate plants and sometimes together; they are wind pollinated. Dry, rather nut-like fruits are produced in the autumn. The aromatic leaves were formerly used for flavouring ale and mead, and were also kept amongst linen to repel moths. *Myrica gale* is found in north-west Europe, as far south as north-west Spain, and east to central Germany and north-west Russia.

Bog Myrtle or Sweet Gale

Devil's Bit Scabious photographed August 16

Golden Rod

Solidago virgaurea (Daisy family) is common in heathy places, on grassy banks and in open woods. It is a perennial, producing several stems up to a height of about 50 cm, flowering from July to September. It is found throughout the British Isles, but is commonest in the extreme south-east and west of the country, and in western Ireland. It is found throughout Europe except on some islands. It is very variable in height, hairiness, leaf shape and in size of its flower heads.

Devil's Bit Scabious, *Succisa pratensis*, is found in the same sorts of places as Golden Rod, and flowers at the same time. It is a perennial, with stems usually around 30 cm high, and round purplish-blue heads of flowers on upright stems. It is common throughout the British Isles and Europe except the far north and the Mediterranean Islands. A pink-flowered form is occasionally found among the normal purple; the flower heads are of two sizes, larger hermaphrodite ones at the apex of the stem, smaller, all-female ones on the branches. Butterflies love them.

Golden Rod photographed August 13

Hieraceum trichocaulon

Hawkweeds

Hieraceum species (Daisy family) are dandelion-flowered plants and may be recognised by their hairy stems, and undivided or toothed leaves. Most of the hairs are long and rather soft, and some may have glandular tips. The pappus hairs are brownish and not feathery.

Common Hawkweed, *Hieraceum vulgatum* is the commonest species in the north of England, Scotland and north Wales, flowering from June to August. It has a basal rosette of stalked leaves, often purple beneath, at flowering time, and a branched flowering stalk with 1–3 stem leaves.

H. umbellatum is common on acid soils, especially in the south of England. It has no basal rosette and numerous narrow stem leaves. *H. perpropinquum* has numerous ovate shallowly toothed leaves diminishing in size up the stem.

H. trichocaulon is common on sandy soils in south-east England. It has 6–15 stem leaves, decreasing in size from the ground, and 5–20 flowers, on the stem.

Common Hawkweed photographed July 26

Western Gorse, Dartmoor August 8

Gorse, Furze or Whin

Three species of Gorse (Pea family) are found on heaths and hills in the British Isles. The commonest is **Gorse**, *Ulex europaens*, which makes a large shrub up to 3 metres high, flowering mainly in spring, but intermittently through the rest of the year, so that the saying goes 'when the gorse is out of flower, kissing is out of fashion'. Gorse is found wild throughout the British Isles, but in Europe only as far east as Italy and Germany, though it is naturalised further east. The other two species are rarer, and flower in late summer. **Dwarf Gorse**, *Ulex minor*, up to 100 cm high, is confined to south-eastern England west to Portland Bill. **Western Gorse**, *Ulex gallii*, up to 150 cm high, is found in western England, south-west Scotland and around the south of Ireland and in the Mourne Mountains: the two species overlap only in southern England and East Anglia. *U. gallii* differs from *U. minor* in its stouter and larger spines, deeper yellow flowers and its longer calyx, 10–13 mm (6–10 mm in *U. minor*).

Dwarf Gorse

Sneezewort photographed August 18

Sneezewort

Achillea ptarmica (Daisy family) is a slender perennial common in wet, grassy places and by rivers on both acid and slightly alkaline soils, and on heathland, throughout the British Isles and most of Europe except the south, eastwards to the Caucaus and Siberia. It flowers in July and August. The common name alludes to the use, in the past, of an infusion of its leaves and flowers.

Marsh Ragwort, *Senecio aquaticus* (Daisy family), grows in somewhat similar places, especially along rivers and in damp meadows, flowering in July and August. It is common throughout the British Isles and most of Europe, especially in the north and west, though absent from much of the Scottish Highlands, Finland and Russia. It is a biennial, up to 80 cm high, and can be distinguished from common Ragwort (*S. jacobaea*) which prefers drier places, by its looser softer branches, and yellow flowers which are not in a flat-topped inflorescence.

144

Sneezewort

Reindeer Moss

Lichens

Reindeer Moss, *Cladonia rangeriferina*, is uncommon in the mountains of Scotland and Wales, but is common in the arctic and sub-arctic regions. In winter it forms the major component of reindeer and caribou food. It is up to 8 cm in height.

Cladonia floerkeana is common on peaty soils of moors and heaths. The red 'matchstick' ends to the branches are the spore-producing bodies; the basal scales form only scattered patches. It is only 2 or 3 cm high.

Cladonia coccifera is common on moors and hills especially at higher altitudes. It forms small patches of scales; the spore-producing bodies are the reddish edges on the cups. It grows up to around 2 cm.

Cladonia floerkeana, Cladonia coccifera

Stags-horn Club Moss photographed August 12

Stags-horn Club Moss

Lycopodium clavatum (Club moss family) is found creeping through mosses or across bare peat, usually underneath a cover of heather, on rather dry, peaty soils. It was formerly found throughout the British Isles, but is now extinct in East Anglia and much of central England. The spore-bearing cones are produced in summer in pairs on narrow, upright stems up to 25 cm high with tightly appressed leaves. Similar but confined to the Scottish Highlands and the Lake District is the Interrupted Clubmoss, *Lycopodium annotinum*. It has cones at the end of upright stems with normal spreading leaves. Marsh Clubmoss, *Lycopodiella inundata* (syn. *Lepidotis inundata*) grows in very wet bogs and is common only in Surrey and the New Forest, though found also in Devon, the Lake District, Scotland and Connemara. *Diphasium alpinum* (syn. *Lycopodium alpinum*) the Alpine Clubmoss, is a smaller, more branching plant with bluish-green fans of shoots. It is found on heaths and in moorland mainly in the mountains in Wales, the Lake District, Scotland and Ireland.

Stags-horn Club Moss

Polytrichum commune photographed May 6

Mosses

Polytrichum commune (Polytrichum family) is one of the largest mosses native in the British Isles, forming hummocks up to 1 metre or more across with stems which are around 20 cm long, and tough and wiry at the base. The spore capsules are on stalks 6–12 cm long. It usually grows on damp moorland or in marshes, often with sphagnum and clumps of rushes, and requires a very acid soil. Other species of *Polytrichum* are shorter; *P. formosum* is commoner in woods and hedges; *P. juniperinum* is a short plant less than 6 cm high, making wide mats in heathland especially in bare places which have been recently burnt. The starry male 'flowers' are often conspicuous, and may be orange or red. *Leucobryum glaucum* (Dicranum family) is another common conspicuous moss on acid soil, found in bogs, heaths and open woods. It forms dense hummocks, pale greyish-green when wet, almost white when dry; capsules are only rarely seen.

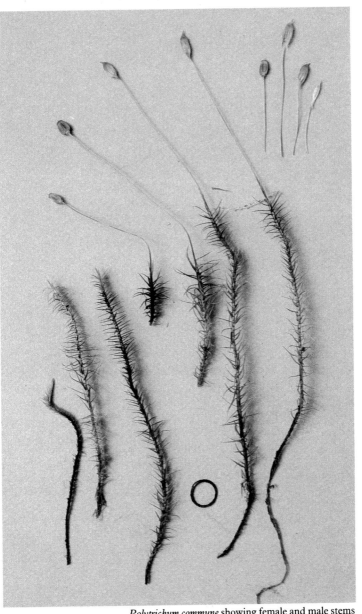

Polytrichum commune showing female and male stems

A Sphagnum bog

Sphagnum Moss

Sphagnum species are common, and often dominant, mosses on wet peaty soils, often forming dense soft cushions of bright green, brown or red. Numerous stems arise from the peat, with branches in scattered whorls, topped by a rosette of branches. The scale-like leaves have two types of cells, one green and one clear and these give the moss its unique water-holding properties. When dry, Sphagnums turn white and dead-looking, but soon go green when watered.

Each species has its own habitat preferences, some growing on relatively dry hummocks, some growing in bog pools and producing aquatic forms. The different species are difficult to identify, but a range of species is shown here.

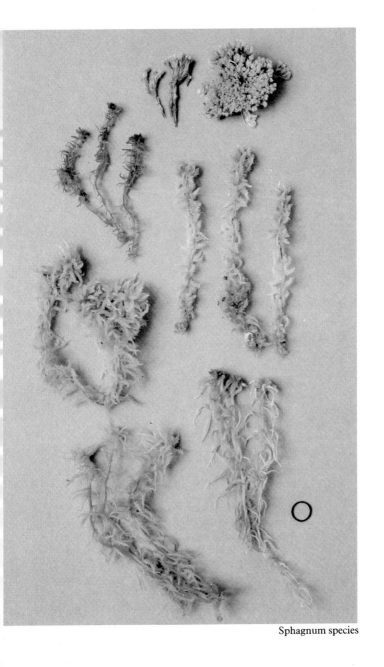

Sphagnum species

Bracken photographed August 11

Bracken

Pteridium aquilinum is the commonest fern in the British Isles, found everywhere on acid soils and often covering large areas of sandy ground or hillsides, shading out all other plants except occasional grasses and Heath Bedstraw (see page 26). It spreads underground by creeping rhizomes, so a single plant can cover a large area. The fronds are up to 2 metres high or more in favourable places; while unfurling they contain cyanide, probably as a defence against grasing, as well as other poisons including carcinogens. Bracken is also the only fern to possess nectaries, to attract ants which deter other, harmful, animals. Outside the British Isles bracken is one of the commonest of all plants, being found everywhere except for southern South America and the Arctic.

Hard Fern, *Blechorum spicant*, is a rather small tufted plant up to 50 cm tall, with simply pinnate sterile fronds and narrower fertile fronds. It is found throughout the British Isles except in central England, in Europe and around the Northern Hemisphere.

154

Hard Fern photographed August 11

Golden-scaled Male Fern

Golden-scaled Male Fern

Dryopteris affinis (syn. *D. borreri*, *D. pseudomas*) is a common fern of acid soils, both in woods and on open moorland, where large clumps of it can be most conspicuous in spring as the golden-brown, scaly fronds unfurl. It is found throughout the British Isles, but is commonest in the west and north. The dense covering of thick golden scales on the central stripe distinguish *D. affinis* from *D. filiximas* and *D. oreades*, the former commonest in lowland woods, the latter on mountains. **Narrow Buckler Fern,** *D. carthusiana* (syn. *D. spinulosa*, *D. lanceolato-cristata*), is characteristic of wet marshes and open alder woods, throughout the British Isles; it has pale green leaves and rather narrow, upright bipinnate fronds with the pinnate pointing upwards, from 40–80 cm tall. Broad Buckler Fern, *D. dilatata*, with dark green, broader leaves, is often found in the same habitats though in drier spots on hummocks, and is also common on mountain-sides and by streams. **Lady Fern,** *Athyrium felix-femina*, is common in damp woods and hedges throughout Britain, usually on acid soils.

Lady Fern

INDEX

Other titles in this series:

Roger Phillips has pioneered the photography of natural history which ensures reliable identification. By placing each specimen against a plain background he is able to show details that would otherwise have been lost if it had been photographed solely *in situ*. Such is the success of this technique that his books, which include *Mushrooms*, *Wild Food* and *Freshwater Fish*, have sold over a million copies worldwide. He is also the winner of numerous awards, including three for best produced and best designed books and the André Simon prize for 1983 for *Wild Food*.

Martyn Rix took a degree in botany at Trinity College, Dublin and then went on to Cambridge. After a further period of study in Zurich he became resident botanist at the Royal Horticultural Society's gardens at Wisley for several years. He is now a freelance writer.

Jacqui Hurst studied photography at Gloucester College of Art & Design, worked as an assistant to Roger Phillips for 4 years, and is now a freelance journalist and photographer, specialising in country matters.

Acknowledgements

We should particularly like to thank Alison Morton, Roger Whitfield, Jack and Selina Grasse, and Dorothy Paish. We are also very grateful to Jill Bryan for her help with the layout and production of the books.

ELM TREE BOOKS
Published by the Penguin Group
27 Wrights Lane, London W8 5TZ, England
Viking Penguin Inc., 40 West 23rd Street, New York, New York 10010, USA
Penguin Books Australia Ltd, Ringwood, Victoria, Australia
Penguin Books Canada Ltd, 2801 John Street, Markham, Ontario, Canada L3R 1B4
Penguin Books (NZ) Ltd, 182–190 Wairau Road, Auckland 10, New Zealand
Penguin Books Ltd, Registered Offices: Harmondsworth, Middlesex, England
First published in Great Britain 1988 by Elm Tree Books
Copyright © 1988 by Roger Phillips
All rights reserved.
ISBN 0-241-12433-6
ISBN 0-241-12434-4 Pbk
Printed and bound in Spain by Cayfosa Industria Gráfica, Barcelona